I0624197

BREAKING THROUGH TO LOVE

BY K. L. JOYNER

BREAKING THROUGH TO LOVE is a collection
Of fifty poems that tell a story of the journey that
A heart goes through trying to find love.

No part of this book may be reproduced in any form
Or by any electronic or mechanical means without
Written permission from the author, except for the
Use of brief quotations in a book review.

© Copyright 2024 by K. L. JOYNER
ALL RIGHTS RESERVED

TO MOM,

Everything you said is coming

True.

TABLE OF CONTENTS

TABLE OF CONTENTS

BREAKING THROUGH TO LOVE

The complexity of my life is not hard to see,
But what is, is what's inside of me.
Outside, my armor is as hard as steel,
So easily, are my feelings concealed.

But if there was some way, you could look inside,
You would see that my heart's very much alive.
And my feelings are as fragile, as a thin layer of ice
That's why I must guard them with all of my life.

While I search for someone who can break through steel.
Without cracking the thin layer of ice,
That my heart has revealed.

LET GO OF YOUR LOVE

Let go of your love,
But how can I release my hold?
Knowing that the essence of my being,
Is connected to your soul.

All that I am,
Is inner twinned in you.
From the moment I first saw you,
My love was true.

Now gaze into my heart,
And tell me I'm a liar.
Say that my love for you,
Isn't still hot, like a fire.

Let go of your love,
Now how can I relinquish my hold?
When it's the love from your heart,
That's the food for my soul.

SEARCHING FOR LOVE

I search for a love,
That will make me strong.
And on cold nights,
Will keep me warm.

Whose heart is as big,
And as tender as mine.
Whose soul is controlled,
By the Divine.

Whose eyes see,
The true treasure is life.
And no wealth on the Earth,
Is worth its price.

I know there are many,
Who think like I do,
And as long as you live,
I'll search for you.

REMEMBERING LOVE

Remember love,
When your face is no longer young,
But old like an ancient mask.
When life has lost its sweetness,
And only the bitterness seems to last.

When hands that once held softness,
Now are hard and cold.
And a voice that used to hold laughter,
Is mute to every sole.

When men were all around you,
To answer your every call.
And would stand in line,
Just to catch your hanky,
If you dared to let it fall.

Remember, remember,
Now that's all you can do.
Because, if you never chose love,
How could it have chosen you?

FORGET YOUR LOVE

Forget your love,
Because I've become old,
And the touch of my skin,
Is like the touch of the cold.

Because now I walk,
With the aid of a cane,
You think my love for you,
No longer remains?

Rip open my chest,
And look at my heart.
It's my love for you,
That gives it its spark.

Forget your love?
How can that be?
How can a tree forget the leaves?
As they fall from thee.

Never my love,
Not even in death.
I live for your love,
And nothing less.

BURNING LOVE

Hear Ye, Hear Ye!
Words spoken in the dark.
Once transferred through the mind,
They bring a spark to the heart.

And with that first initial spark,
That bursts into a flame,
Heat flows through the body,
Cancelling out, the bitter pain.

Some, call it love,
Others call it joy.
Like the kind a woman feels,
When she gives birth,
To a baby girl,
Or a baby boy.

But in the end,
It's all the same,
You get out of love,
What you put into, the flame.

MISSING YOU

As the days slowly pass me by,
I find myself wondering why.
The thoughts of you still drive me mad,
And remembering your touch makes me sad.

Then in a flash, it's there, in my mind.
It's the want of your love,
That still drives my heart,
And knowing I can't have it,
Is tearing me apart.

But in the dark of the night,
I lay down with a smile.
Because our love will last a lifetime,
And our anger, only a little while.

REMEMBER ME

Remember me,
Remember my time.
Remember my face,
Body, and Mind.

Remember my love for you,
It was as strong as steel.
I gave you my heart,
And everything, it could feel.

But you gave me nothing,
Nothing in return.
Only lies and deceit,
Many times, I got burned.

Now, I've moved past you,
And once again, I'm strong.
You told me I was a dreamer,
But now, my dreams, live on.

LIVE, LIFE

As the sun bursts through the morning sky,
I find myself wondering why.
The search for love often ends in pain,
Just as the need for wealth drives the rich insane.

Some call these human qualities a curse,
That can only end as a worthless birth.
While others say they are a blessing,
That makes us appreciate life's little lessons.

Whether they are wrong or right,
There is nothing more fragile than life.
It can leave us any day or night,
So, we must always treat it right.

Enjoy everything it offers,
It's joy and its pains.
Because once it's gone,
Nothing more will remain.

ETERNAL LOVE

My love,
I'm lost in the maze,
Of your heart.

And even though I'm scared,
I refuse to stop.
Wandering aimlessly, through your halls,
I hear the whispers of your passions,
And the secrets they hold.

They want a man,
Who's strong, but tender.
Whose heart can break,
But he'll never surrender.

The love she pours into his heart,
And even when it's filled,
She can never stop.

As I ponder on my journey,
I thank the Heavens above,
For letting me find,
My Eternal Love.

MY FRIEND

Curled up like a rose,
That needs to be opened.
Your heart has been closed,
It has also been broken.

When there were many,
They were few.
When there was love,
There was only you.

There in the beginning,
And still, to the end.
My Lover, My Wife
And Finally, My Friend.

LOVE SOMEBODY

The success of a man,
Or his prosperity in life.
Lies in the strength,
Of his woman or wife.

So, if you ever meet someone,
Who has done it alone,
He is simply a king,
Without a throne.

And a king,
Without a queen or throne,
Is a hollowed man,
Who will end life alone.

SAY IT

We both love each other,
That's clear to our hearts,
But I cherish your words,
When you speak them in the dark.

They flow through my ears,
And across my mind,
And I will never stop them,
Not after a lifetime.

I love you,
Rings clear to my soul,
And my heart yearns for the words,
As they unfold.

So, if you just think them,
That's fine.
But once in a while,
Let the words run through my mind.

HELLO LOVE

Hello love,
I searched for you every day.
I'm glad you finally came my way,
Of all the people in the world,
You were, that special girl.

I recognized you from the start,
You sent a signal to my heart.
You made it clear, in every way,
That you too, were looking, every day.

Now that we're finally,
Face to face.
I look forward to your warm embrace.

LISTENING FOR LOVE

Listen people I'll make this fast,
Life is short and not meant to last.
So, those whom you hold dear in your heart,
Show the love from the very start.

You may think they're plenty of time,
But life is controlled by the Divine.
Just when you think it's starting to begin,
Can be when you find yourself, at its end.

So, never leave love untold,
Whether you're young or very old.
Because the preciousness of the word,
Is somehow devalued, when never heard.

So, you must say it, loud and clear,
But to the heart, not to the ear.

PERFECTION

Perfection,
I saw it the other day.
I saw it when you came my way.

Your physical attributes,
Were complete.
But something more wonderful,
Lies beneath.

I couldn't even make a sound,
Though my heart was heard,
For miles around.

How could someone in my place,
Talk to an angel of another race.

Perfection is beauty in a glass,
But on humans, it will never last.

So, to make your life more complete,
Look for the something,
That lies beneath.

CAN'T LET GO

Here I am again today,
I just can't seem to stay away.

It's a year since you've been gone,
But still, I call the house our home.
Your clothes are where you let them lay,
I touch them every single day.

Sometimes in the dead of night,
I cry while holding your pillow tight.
The scent of you still remains,
And it adds agony to bitter pain.

I know what you said that last night,
Before the Lord took your life.
You said, "I would have to live on,"
And I've tried to be strong.

But my heart can't tell a lie,
I will love you until I die.

LOST IN THE HEART

A follower of the heart,
Must sometimes travel in the dark.
Of course, there's light,
To the left or right.

But if you turn to go that away,
Then off the road, you will stray.
Now to follow the heart is fine,
But it's better, to follow the mind.

Because easily,
The heart goes astray.
When the other is headed,
Another way.

TEARS

My eyes are wet, and I don't know why,
Even the day she left, I refused to cry.
It hurt me like I've never been hurt before,
If this here is love, Then I don't want it anymore.

Baby if you're out there, and you hear my plea,
Please, stop this pain, by coming back to me.

Now, I know I've done many things wrong,
But without your love, I just can't go on.
Now listen to reason and hear my call,
Because without your love, I feel nothing at all.

RISK IT ALL

People wonder why I cry,
I don't speak, just pass them by,
The pain is too strong for me to convey,
If I could, it might pass away.

Then I would be left with nothing at all,
And into that pit, I would fall.
But pain is a feeling, that I would risk,
For the chance of your love, that's eternal bliss.

SEEDS OF THE HEART

Love grows in shallow grass,
For the seeds of the heart,
Take root fast.

And reaches quickly into the souls,
Of both, the young, and the old.
And if we were to tend this fertile ground,
True love would sprout, where none was found.

IT'S MONDAY AGAIN

It's Monday again and you're still gone,
I guess our love wasn't that strong.
I remember the vows we took at the church,
There they lie, with their face in the dirt.

You didn't even tell me why,
Couldn't say another lie.
I'm not mad, I understand,
It's not me, It's Monday again.

THE HEARTS SPEAKS

The heart speaks,
When the mouth is mute.
Love grows only in truth.

When the Gods,
Have all had their due,
And fate plays his final trick on you.

Will you be ready to face the light,
Or is Heaven and Hell merely a fight?
One that's not young, but very old,
And not between Angels, but between Souls.

If there be judging, be it from within,
For, if Heaven be the paradise,
Then Earth, be the Sin.

REMEMBERING

The rain fell on my windowpane,
And again, I thought I would go insane.
It's been three years since she's been gone,
But still, I expect to see her every morning.

Sometimes, I see her on the streets,
In the faces of different people that I meet.
But I know it's a lie,
Because I was there that day,
I saw her die.

There was nothing I could do,
It happened just that fast.
I remember the gun,
I saw the mask.

If you love someone in your life,
Whether it be a friend, a Girl, or a Wife.

Never let a moment pass,
That you don't treat like your last.
Because if you do, you may miss out,
On what life is all about.

IT'S OVER, BUT IT'S NOT

The sadness of this day may never pass,
So, to get by, I must wear a mask.
For love has an angel's face,
But a devil's fire, once it's erased.

So, to protect myself,
From the pains of the heart.
I must choose wisely,
When searching for love, from the start.

There are many phases of love,
That come and pass,
True love is the one,
That comes and lasts.

So, if love has come and gone,
And you feel like you can't go on.
Then you can mourn, but make it fast,
Because true love is out there,
And it will last.

LIVING AGAIN

It's another day and I'm all alone,
Thinking about you, might use the phone.
But I said I wouldn't call,
Because if I do, then I might fall.

Back in love, and that won't do.
Because I remember the pain,
Of leaving you.

It took courage, and there was pain.
But it will take more, to live again.

BROKEN UP

My eyes are wet, and I don't know why,
Even the day she left, I refused to cry.

She said it wouldn't happen again,
And this time it happened with a friend.
I still don't know what I did wrong,
I thought our love was so strong.

Sometimes, I see her on the street,
And turn corners fast, so we don't meet.
The tears my eyes shed every day,
Are drops of a life, that she threw away.

CHANGE OF HEART

Under the stars of eternal bliss,
Young lovers have stared and cast their wish.
Most of the time it would be the same,
They always wanted their love to remain.

Strong and powerful, like in the start.
With a calling so clear, it controlled the heart.

Though many times, that wish was cast,
On very few, did it last.

If you are looking for someone to blame,
Look to the heart, who made a change.

BROKEN WING

Easily broken, like a butterfly's wing
The heart is a very fragile thing.

You must use care, to keep out every crack.
Because love will seep out, once you do that.

And just like that wing, that was broken.
Maybe that crack is a token,
A small reminder to the mind,
So, it can stop the heart in time.

Before that crack, becomes a gash.
And true love is thrown to the ground,
And smashed.

SINCERITY

Sincerity is a kiss,
That's neither pungent nor sweet,
And its passion is marked,
By a quickened heartbeat.

Its roots dig deep,
Until they pierce the heart.
Drawing blood.
And there's no fighting it,
When it's mixed with love.

Still, there are many,
Who refuse to see,
That sincerity is truth,
Multiplied by three.

Now,
No more talk,
Not another word shall be spoken.

I will prove my sincerity to you,
Let me start now.
By giving you a lifetime,
That's filled with, my love, and devotion.

SHE'S LOOKING AGAIN

She's looking at me again that way,
My heart's beating so fast,
I don't know what to say.

Should I smile or maybe smirk,
Anything, except act like a jerk.

This coming of age is driving me mad.
I find myself happy, I find myself sad.
How could it be, that just her glance?
Can send my heart, into a dance?

This feeling is reaching, clear to my toes.
It's making me dizzy.
It's making me bold.

Next time she looks, I'll look back.
Then both our hearts, will know where there at.

MADE IN HEAVEN

To say I love you, would be a shallow thing to say,
But rather, my heart would cry if you went away.
Because I never thought I would meet,
Someone who made my life so complete.

Your love is embedded in my heart like a stone,
And without you, I could not go on.

Though your physical appearance is a gift from above,
Your inner beauty is blind, to all, but love.
Even as time plays its wicked game,
We will forever, remain the same.

And when the time comes for one of us, to say goodbye.
The other shouldn't think to cry,
Because a love this strong, here on Earth
Must have had a Heavenly birth.

GETTING OVER LOVE

When love is over,
There's nothing to say,
It's best to go your separate ways.
You can pretend, but in the end,
Love has gone away.

If you try to live the lie,
That everything's okay.
The pain inside, that you try to hide,
Will grow stronger every day.

Face the loss of this love,
With your heart intact.
Then after the pain has come and gone,
Your heart can still react.

TIME

Time is something beyond our control,
It affects the young as well as the old.

So, spend every second of your time,
Using your, Heart, Soul, and Mind.

Now, I will show you where to start,
Let me begin, with Your Heart.

REBUILDING LOVE

The crumbled ruins of the house,
Was abandoned by all,
But a mouse.

But if he chose to stand his ground,
Then soon there would be many,
All around.

Just like the ruins of a heart,
Though love has been torn apart.

If you choose to stand your ground,
A stronger love will be found.

One that's built within the heart,
And no storm can tear it apart.

NIBBLING ON LOVE

When your nostrils first sniff,
The scent of love.
You must take care, to find out,
If it's from below or above.

A love from above,
Has the sweetest taste.
But a love from below,
Is bitter to all it embraces.

So, when you eat sweet love,
Nibble on it slow.
I know it's true sweetness,
Demands that you eat it fast.

But if it's sour,
And bitter to the taste.
You may bite it once,
But it will never be embraced.

Sweet love is different,
It's from the Divine.
But eat it very slowly,
It must last, your entire lifetime.

CAT'S EYE

Eyes like a cat,
That pierce you to your soul.
A body like a lioness,
That's beyond your control.

A heart that beats,
Twice the speed of sound.
A love that's like oxygen,
All around.

Gaze upon her face,
And it will drive you mad.
The touch of her skin,
Will burn you bad.

If you see her,
Don't make a sound.
Because, wherever she's at,
Love is always around.

WHO

See my body, feel my heat.
Touch my soul, make me complete.

With your heart, break my chains.
Give me the power, to love again.

Feel the sun, on my face.
The heat doesn't burn, it penetrates.

In the end, everything is the same.
All you need is to know my name.

I LOVE YOU

If you say it,
Say it slow.
So, both, my Heart, and Mind,
Will know.

It's there in your face,
I can see it,
Every trace.

I never thought,
That it would come.
First, it walked,
Now, it runs.

Through the thick,
Forrest of life.
You have come,
To be my wife.

There's no need,
To say a word.
Because my heart,
Has already heard.

TREASURE

Treasure you, treasure me,
Treasure happiness, treasure sorrow,
Treasure today, treasure tomorrow.

Treasure everything you see,
Treasure everything you touch.
Treasure everything you want,
Treasure everything you lust.

You can treasure,
All these things,
But in the end,
You treasure in vain.

Treasure life,
Until its end.

Because it's the only thing.
We spend.

THE LIGHT OF LOVE

There are many things to love,
When you are a child.
Like the love of a puppy,
You thought, came from the wild.

Like the love of a blanket,
That kept you warm through the night.
Or the love of a buddy,
Who became your friend for life.

But now you're grown,
And things have changed,
But love will forever,
Remain the same.

It's a force,
Beyond our control.
That's why when it comes,
We can't stop its hold.

It merges heart,
That were apart.
Bringing light,
Where there was dark.

I WISH

I wish,
That wishes did come true.
Then my life would be spent,
Loving, only you.

So, if you're listening,
Anyone above.
I cast this wish,
In the name of love.

Through all the loneliness,
In this world.
I pray it finds,
One special girl.

There's no need,
To mention her name.
Because the wish I cast,
She cast, the same.

HEART PLUS MIND EQUALS LIFETIME

I listened to my heart,
And it spoke your name.
Now I have been forever changed.

It said, "that our love is stronger,
Than distance or time.
Because true love is given,
When hearts, meet minds.

So, open up mentally,
And let me in,
So, true love can start,
And never end."

LOVE TALKER

She said, "I talked in my sleep,"
And the words, she would repeat.

"I love you,
When the sky is blue.
I love you,
In the morning dew.

These are just,
A few of the ways.
Because I praise your love,
All my days.

Even when,
I'm dead and gone.
I'll praise your love,
On and on."

These words you spoke,
In your sleep.
No wonder my life's,
So complete.

LOVE IS

What is love?
Love is timeless,
Love is friends,
Love is feelings,
That never ends.

Love is me,
Love is you.
Whether we're together,
Or apart.

Love is buried deeply,
In both our hearts.

So, don't ever try to understand,
Because love is a gift,
From the Lord's Hand.

LOVE

Love,
What can I say?
It's something that happens,
Every day.

But when it happens,
And it's complete.
It turns into a force,
In which, none can compete.

It drives hearts,
To the brink of joy,
And will not be stopped,
Even when death is deployed.

So, when faced with this love,
Just surrender your heart.
Because the battle was over,
From the magical start.

AN OLD MAN'S TRUTH

I loved a woman long ago,
When she stopped loving me, I don't know.
We still live as husband and wife,
And probably will, for the rest of our life.

I say life because we're bonded as one,
We took that oath, under The Father, and The Son.
We said, "We'd last through time and space,"
But the years have erased our love, without a trace.

I look at her sometimes, and I remember the past,
And love comes back, like an explosive blast.
Back, with memories of holding hands,
And taking long walks, on the sand.

Though time has been an enemy, to the bitter end.
Her love has really, been a tender friend.

So, forget all the things, an old man said,
Because without that woman's love,
I would have, long been, dead.

QUEEN

I gaze into the eyes of a queen every day,
But when she gazes back, I have nothing to say.
Instead, I find myself nervous, I find myself shy,
I find myself joking, just to get by.

Maybe, it's the way the sun sparkles in her eyes,
Or, the way she glances at me when she walks by.
That transports me, back to a place in time,
When queens were all around me, and they were all mine.

But those were the foolish days of my past,
And just like those queens, they didn't last.

So, to find a queen for your heart,
You must be a king, from the very start.

A MOTHER'S LOVE

Though I murdered it,
At an early age.
It resurrected itself,
Back from the grave.

I have escaped it,
Many times.
But me, it always,
Seems to find.

It's a gift,
Of which, I'm unworthy.
All I offer it is pain,
And it has consumed it, again, and again.

And still, it flows,
Back in, like the tide,
And will, continue to do so,
Even after, she's died.

A FATHER'S LOVE

He never spoke,
The words that I wanted,
To hear.

But, in his actions,
They were quite clear.

Hard as oak, was his heart.
He refused emotions,
Even in the dark.

He never told me,
The duties of a man,
But growing through him,
I understand.

No longer a child,
I see with my soul,
That the hardness of his heart,
Was simply a shield.

That kept the warmth of his love,
Safely, concealed.

www.ingramcontent.com/pod-product-compliance
Lightning Source LLC
Chambersburg PA
CBHW020343130626
46549CB00003B/1274